Sarah Quartel Songbook

10 songs for upper voices

MUSIC DEPARTMENT
OXFORD
UNIVERSITY PRESS

OXFORD
UNIVERSITY PRESS

Great Clarendon Street, Oxford OX2 6DP,
United Kingdom

Oxford University Press is a department of the University of Oxford.
It furthers the University's objective of excellence in research, scholarship,
and education by publishing worldwide. Oxford is a registered trade mark of
Oxford University Press in the UK and in certain other countries

First published 2021

ISBN 978-0-19-355105-3

Music and text origination by Katie Johnston
Printed in Great Britain on acid-free paper by
Halstan & Co. Ltd, Amersham, Bucks.

Contents

Introduction	iv
Songbird	1
I remember	12
The Birds' Lullaby	21
All the way home	28
In time of silver rain	35
As you sing	38
All shall be well	49
All shall be well, violin part	63
Sing, my Child	66
Refuge	73
Voice on the Wind	81

Introduction

It is such a pleasure to see these pieces together in one collection. The oldest selection, 'Songbird', was written in my early 20s for the choir of close friends in which I sang. 'I remember' and 'In time of silver rain' were commissioned by a tightknit group of women in a rural community near my hometown. 'All the way home' and 'As you sing' were two of my first pieces written for choirs in England. The texts of these songs were inspired by messages I received from the commissioning choirs describing the joy of singing in their choral communities. 'The Birds' Lullaby' holds a special place in my heart, as it was a commissioned gift from a husband to his treasured wife and her choir. The Peninsula Girls Chorus of California premiered 'Voice on the Wind' in 2014, and, in 2016, 'Sing, my Child' was premiered by a group of nearly 500 singers at the International Choral Kathaumixw in British Columbia.

'Refuge' is a new release that was written in 2020 for the Atlanta Women's Chorus. It received an online premiere in 2021 as a result of the COVID-19 pandemic. 'All shall be well' was written in 2020 for the National Children's Chorus of the United States of America, with a text that was inspired by words shared with me by the choristers after the first wave of COVID-19 lockdowns. These young singers spoke of their choir and choral singing as places for self-care, self-expression, and healing.

As I look at the titles included in this collection and remember the musicians who have inspired them, I am reminded that choral music-making holds a tremendous power to connect and unite us. I am thankful to every person who inspired these pieces and grateful to Robyn Elton and Laura Jones for bringing this collection to life.

Sarah Quartel
March 2021

Songbird

Words and music by
SARAH QUARTEL
(b. 1982)

Duration: 2.5 mins

17 unis. mp
One lit - tle bird on a branch sits fan - ning am - ber wings to the pass - ers - by.
21
Two lit - tle birds in flight_ are thread - ing webs of gold in an end - less sky.
mp
Two lit - tle birds in flight_ are thread - ing webs of gold in an end - less sky.
25 mf
Three lit - tle birds with brush - es paint - ing moon - lit sighs in the height of day.
mf
Three lit - tle birds with brush - es paint - ing moon - lit sighs in the height of day.
29
Four lit - tle birds with voi - ces gleam - ing breathe to the wind sing-ing 'come my way!'
Four lit - tle birds with voi - ces gleam - ing breathe to the wind sing-ing 'come my way!'

* Keyboard reduction for rehearsal only.

41
f
da da da da_ da da da da da da da da_ da da da da da
mf
Five lit-tle birds with fea-thers fluff-ing
f
da da da da_ da da da da da da da da_ da da da da da
mp
doo doo___
f
da da da da_ da da da da da da da da_ da da da da da
mp
doo doo___
f
mf
45
stretch and spread in the mid - day sun.
mp
doo doo___
doo doo___
mf
Six lit - tle birds are coo - ing, hum - ming,
doo doo___ doo doo___

49
doo doo doo doo
mp
drawing the eyes of ev-'ry-one. doo doo
mf
doo doo Sev-en lit-tle birds in foun-tains splash-ing.
53
mf
doo doo Eight lit-tle birds raise voi-ces high-er,
mf
doo doo Eight lit-tle birds raise voi-ces high-er,
(mf)
Drop-lets soar, they fawn and play. Eight lit-tle birds raise voi-ces high-er,

57
breathe to the wind sing-ing, 'come my way!' doo doo doo
f
Sing, lit-tle bird, so sweet - ly.
3
breathe to the wind sing-ing, 'come my way!' doo doo doo

61
sub. mf
da da da da da da da da da da da doo doo doo
sub. f
3
ah
Drown my fears com - plete - ly.
da da da da da da da da da da da doo doo doo

65
da da da da__ da da da da da da da da__ da da da da da da da da da__ da da da da
ah da da da da da__ da da da da
da da da da__ da da da da da da da da__ da da da da da da da da da__ da da da da

68
da da da da__ da da da da da Fly, lit - tle Song-birds, to the ho - ri - zon.
da da da da__ da da da da da Fly, lit - tle Song-birds, to the ho - ri - zon.
da da da da__ da da da da da Fly, lit - tle Song-birds, to the ho - ri - zon.

71
Land meets sky and_ sky meets sea. Dance, lit-tle Song-birds, flick_ your fea - thers,
Land meets sky and_ sky meets sea. Dance, lit-tle Song-birds, flick_ your fea - thers,
Land meets sky and sky meets sea. Dance, lit-tle Song-birds, flick_ your fea - thers,
75
move the cur - rent,_ car - ry me! Sing, lit-tle Song-birds, call to your lov - ers.
move the cur-rent, car - ry me! Sing, lit-tle Song-birds, call to your lov - ers.
move the cur - rent,_ car - ry me! Sing, lit-tle Song-birds, call to your lov - ers.

79
Draw them in com - plete - ly. You, lit-tle Song-birds, you can sing a - ny-thing. I
da da da You, lit-tle Song-birds, you can sing a - ny-thing. I
da da da You, lit-tle Song-birds, you can sing a - ny-thing. I
83
f
fol - low the wind and I come your way, come your way, come your way!
fol - low the wind and I come your way, come your way, come your way!
fol - low the wind and I come your way, come your way, come your way!
f

86
mp
doo doo doo doo doo doo doo doo doo doo doo doo doo doo doo doo doo doo doo
mp
doo doo doo doo doo doo doo doo doo doo doo doo doo doo doo doo doo doo
mp
doo doo doo doo doo doo doo doo doo doo doo doo doo doo doo doo doo
mp
90
p
doo doo doo doo doo doo doo doo doo doo doo doo doo doo doo doo doo doo doo doo
doo doo doo doo doo doo doo doo doo doo doo doo doo doo doo doo doo doo doo
doo doo doo doo doo doo doo doo doo doo doo doo doo doo doo doo doo doo
p

94
__ doo doo doo doo doo doo doo doo doo doo doo doo doo doo doo doo doo doo doo__
p
doo doo__ doo doo doo doo doo doo doo doo doo doo doo doo doo doo doo doo doo
p
doo doo doo doo__ doo doo doo doo doo doo doo doo doo doo doo doo doo doo doo

98
__ doo doo doo doo doo doo doo doo doo doo doo doo doo doo doo doo doo doo
doo doo__ doo doo doo doo doo doo doo doo doo doo doo doo doo doo doo
doo doo doo doo__ doo doo doo doo doo doo doo doo doo doo doo doo doo doo

Commissioned by Sharon Little and the Treble Makers Women's Choir in celebration of their fifth anniversary, and dedicated to women who love to sing

I remember

Words and music by
SARAH QUARTEL

Duration: 4 mins

Also available in versions for unison voices and piano (978–0–19–355084–1), SABar and piano (978–0–19–353481–0), and solo voice and piano (high voice 978–0–19–354952–4/low voice 978–0–19–354953–1).

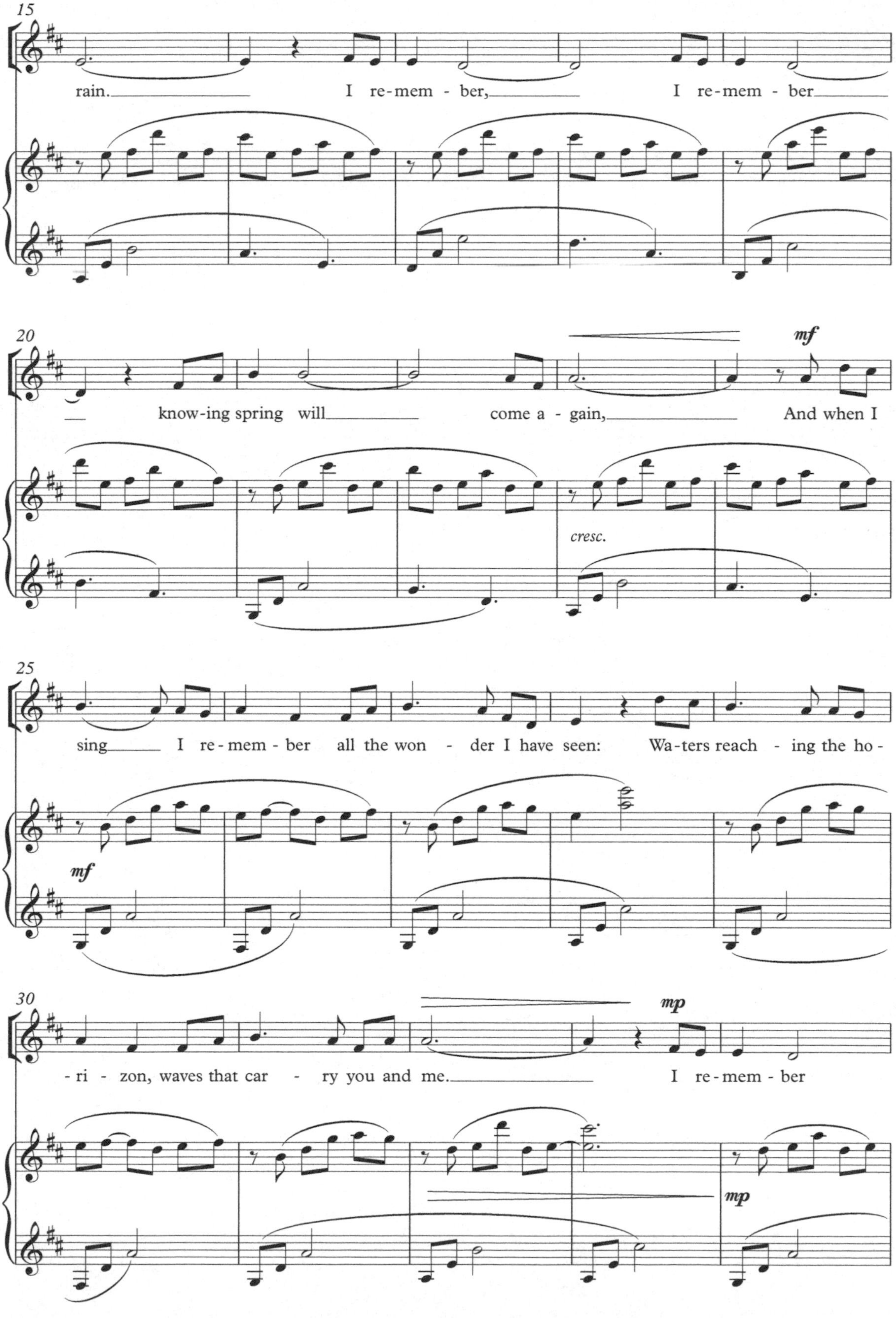
15
rain. I re-mem - ber, I re-mem - ber
20
knowing spring will come a - gain, And when I
mf
cresc.
25
sing I re-mem - ber all the won - der I have seen: Wa-ters reach - ing the ho -
mf
30
- ri - zon, waves that car - ry you and me. I re-mem - ber
mp
mp

35
this, my friend.
39
mp
S.
I re-mem - ber, I re-mem - ber gold-en
mp
A.
I re-mem - ber, I re-mem - ber gold-en
44
sum - mers when corn is high. I re-mem - ber,
sum - mers when corn is high. I re-mem - ber,

49
I re-mem - ber branch-es reach - ing to the
I re-mem - ber branch-es reach - ing to the
54
mf
sky, And when I sing I re-mem - ber all the har - vests of the
mf
sky, And when I sing I re-mem - ber all the har - vests of the
mf
59
field, Fruits of love that lie in wait - ing, all the boun - ty now re - vealed.
field, Fruits of love that lie in wait - ing, all the boun - ty now re - vealed.

64
mp
I re-mem - ber this, my friend.
mp
I re-mem - ber this, my friend.
mp
69
f
In my song there's a race through a wild green
f
ah
f
74
mead - ow, The sun - shine so bright in my eyes. In my
ah

79
mf
song there's a day by the cool of the wa - ter, Know - ing that
mf
ah
ah
mf
84
mp
you're by my side, know - ing that you're by my
mp
ah
mp
89
side a - gain.

94
mp
I re-mem - ber, I re-mem - ber all the
mp
I re-mem - ber, I re-mem - ber all the
mp
99
loved ones I have known. I re-mem - ber,
loved ones I have known. I re-mem - ber,
104
I re-mem - ber all they've taught me, how I've
I re-mem - ber all they've taught me, how I've

109
f
grown. When I sing I re-mem-ber ma-ny lives that share my
f
grown. When I sing I re-mem-ber ma-ny lives that share my
f

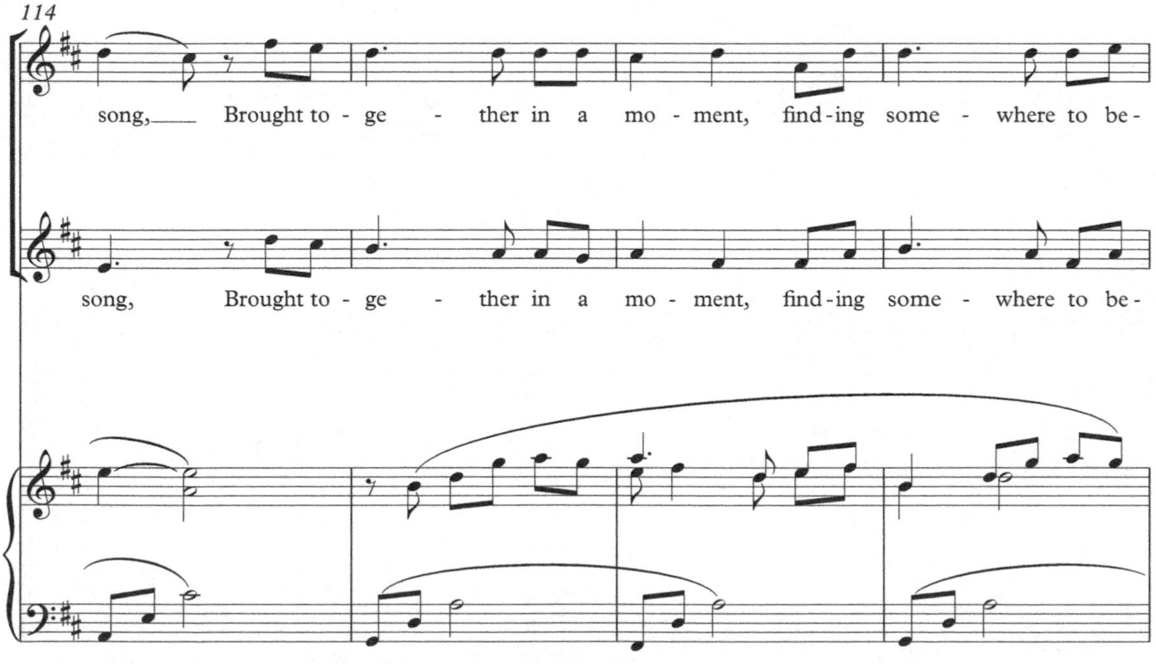
114
song, Brought to-ge - ther in a mo - ment, find-ing some - where to be-
song, Brought to-ge - ther in a mo - ment, find-ing some - where to be-

meno mosso
118
mf
- long, And I re-mem - ber you, my friend.
mf
- long, And I re-mem - ber you, my friend.
meno mosso
mf
rit.
a tempo
123
(unis.)
mp
S./A.
I re-mem - ber you, my friend.
mp
128
rit.

Dedicated, with love, to Andrew Potter,
who commissioned this piece for Jan Spooner Swabey and JuSSt Voices

The Birds' Lullaby

E. Pauline Johnson (1861–1913)

SARAH QUARTEL

Duration: 3 mins

Also available in a version for SATB unaccompanied (978–0–19–354369–0).

13
mf
All day we have ca - rolled and now would be sleep - ing,
mp
doo doo doo doo doo doo doo doo doo doo doo doo doo doo doo doo
mp
doo doo doo doo doo doo doo doo doo doo doo doo doo doo doo doo
17
So e-cho the an - thems we war-bled to you; While we
doo doo doo doo doo doo doo doo you;
doo doo doo doo doo doo doo doo you;
21
swing, And your branch-es sing, And we drowse
Swing, swing, swing, swing, sing, sing, sing, sing, drowse, we drowse
Swing, swing, swing, swing, sing, sing, sing, sing, drowse, we drowse

26
mp
to your dream - - y whis - per-ing.
p
now, dream-y whisp'r - ing.
mp
doo doo doo doo doo doo doo doo
p
now, dream-y whisp'r - ing.
31
Sing to us now, night - wind sigh - ing,
mf
Sing to us, ce - dars; the night - wind is sigh - ing,
mp
Sing to us now, night - wind sigh - ing,
35
woo - ing, plead - ing, you re - ply; da da da
Is woo-ing, is plead - ing, to hear you re - ply;
you re - ply; da da da
woo - ing, plead - ing, you re - ply;

39
mf
in your arms we are ly - ing, da da da da da
f
And here in your arms we are rest - ful - ly ly - ing,
in your arms we are ly - ing, da da da da da
mf
in your arms we are ly - ing,
43
mp
long - ing, dream - ing, lul - la - by; While we
mf
And long-ing to dream to your soft lul - la - by; While we
mp
long - ing, dream - ing, lul - la - by; While we
47
swing, And your branch-es sing, And we
swing, swing, swing, swing, sing, sing, sing, sing,
swing, swing, swing, swing, sing, sing, sing, sing,

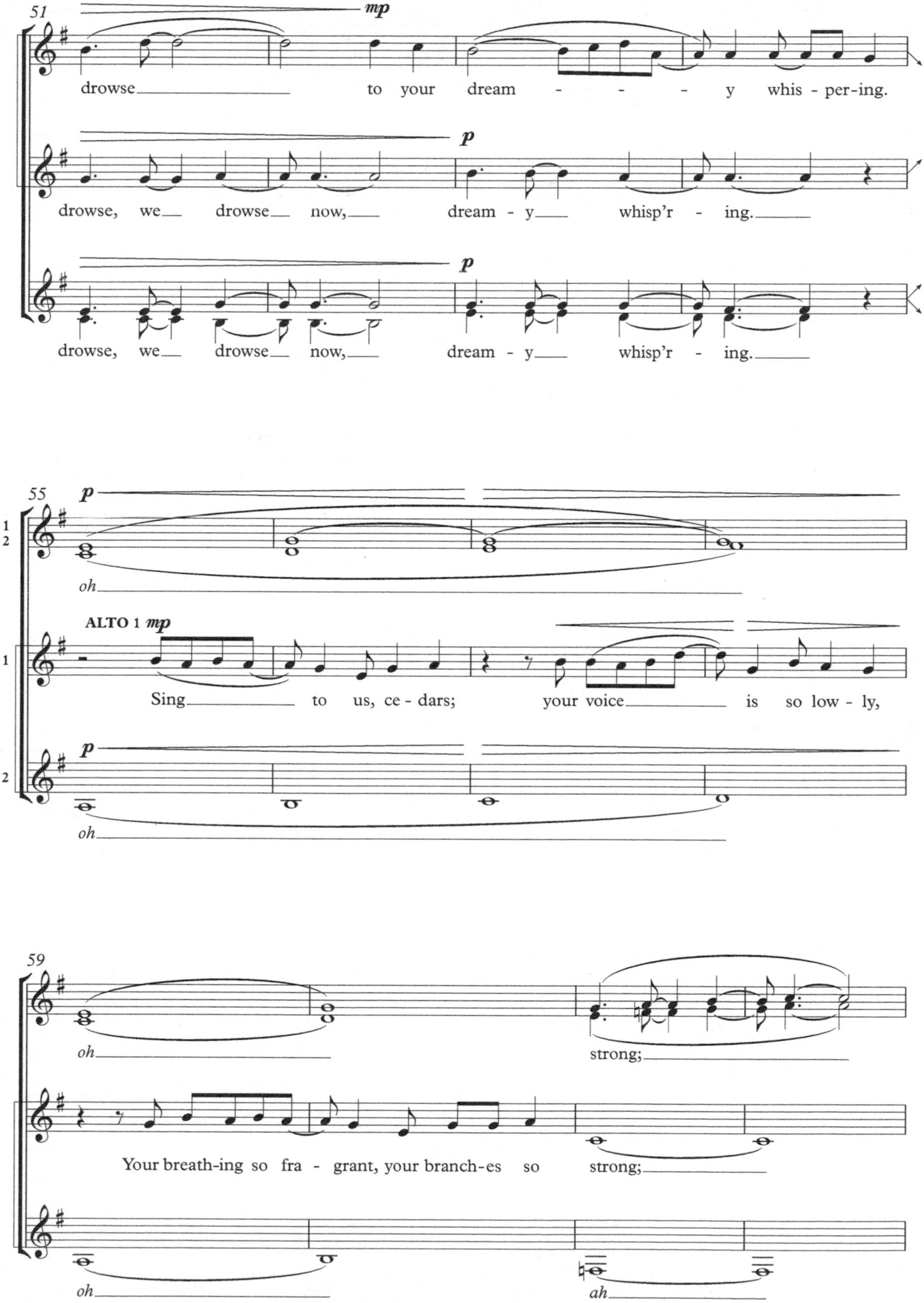
51
mp
drowse to your dream - - - y whis - per-ing.
p
drowse, we drowse now, dream - y whisp'r - ing.
p
drowse, we drowse now, dream - y whisp'r - ing.
55
p
S. 1
S. 2
oh
ALTO 1 mp
A. 1
Sing to us, ce - dars; your voice is so low - ly,
p
A. 2
oh
59
oh
strong;
Your breath-ing so fra - grant, your branch-es so strong;
oh
ah

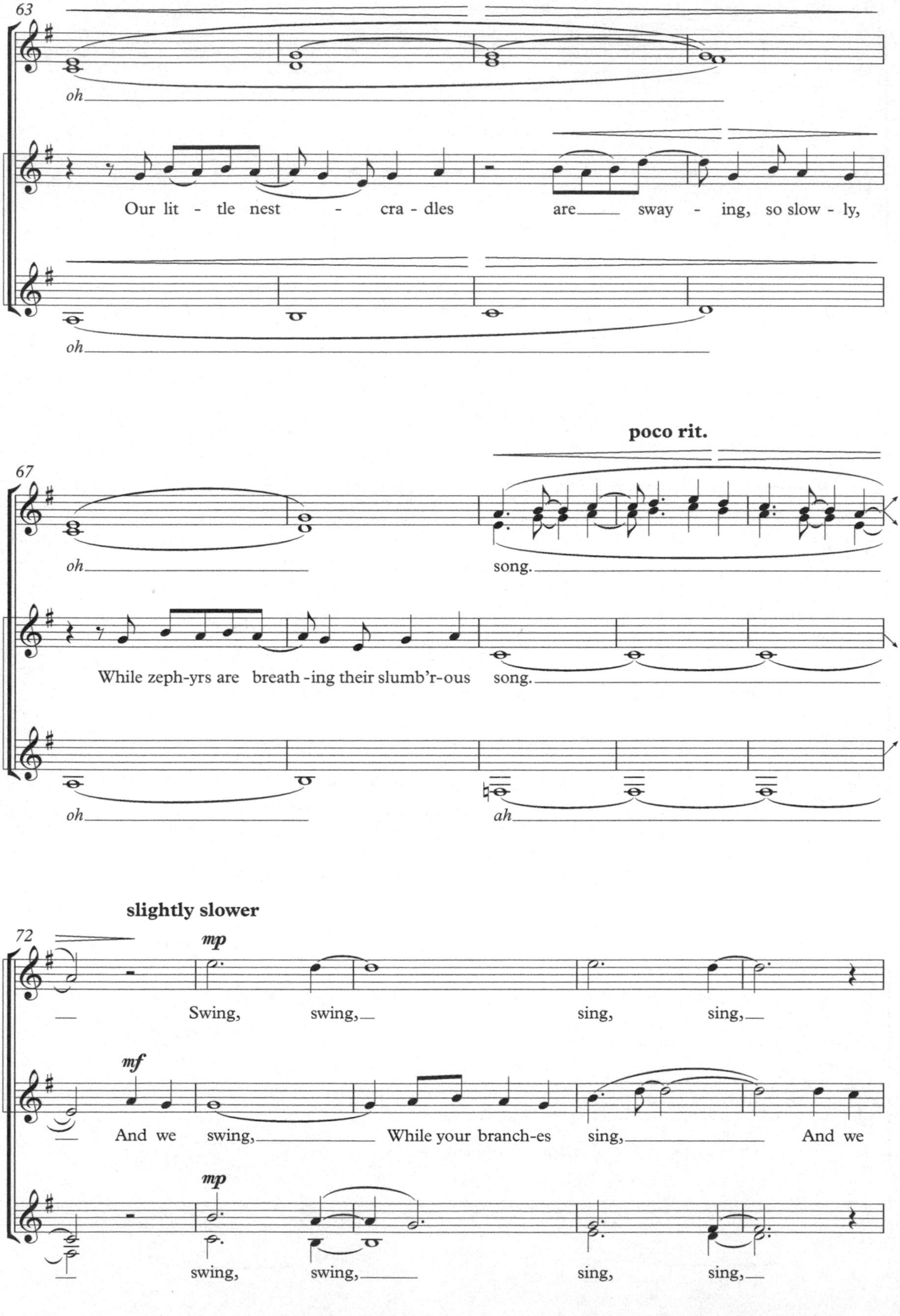
63
oh
Our lit - tle nest - cra - dles are sway - ing, so slow - ly,
oh
poco rit.
67
oh
song.
While zeph-yrs are breath - ing their slumb'r-ous song.
oh
ah
slightly slower
72
S. 1
mp
Swing, swing, sing, sing,
S. 2
mf
And we swing, While your branch-es sing, And we
A. 1
A. 2
mp
swing, swing, sing, sing,

77
f
drowse, drowse, And we swing, swing,
f
drowse, and we drowse, swing, swing,
f
drowse, drowse, swing, swing,
82
poco rit.
mf
While your branch - es sing, And we drowse to your
mp
sing, sing, drowse,
mp
sing, sing, drowse,
87
sempre rit.
mp
dream - y whis-per-ing.
p
doo doo doo doo doo doo
p
oh doo doo doo doo doo doo doo doo doo doo doo
p unis.
oh doo doo doo doo doo doo doo doo doo doo doo

Commissioned by Alex Patterson and the Radcliffe Ladies' Choir
in celebration of the choir's 25th anniversary

All the way home

Text written and inspired by
members of the Radcliffe Ladies' Choir as they
reflected on their moto, "friendship through singing"

SARAH QUARTEL

Duration: 3.5 mins

Also available in versions for SATB and piano (978–0–19–354379–9) and solo voice and piano (high voice 978–0–19–354742–1)/low voice 978–0–19–354743–8).

22
I be - long, joy - ful, with har - mon - ies sing me
29
mf
all the way home with a song in my heart. All the way
mf
35
home bright - en my path and car - ry me on,
42
mp
poco rit.
all the way home.
mp

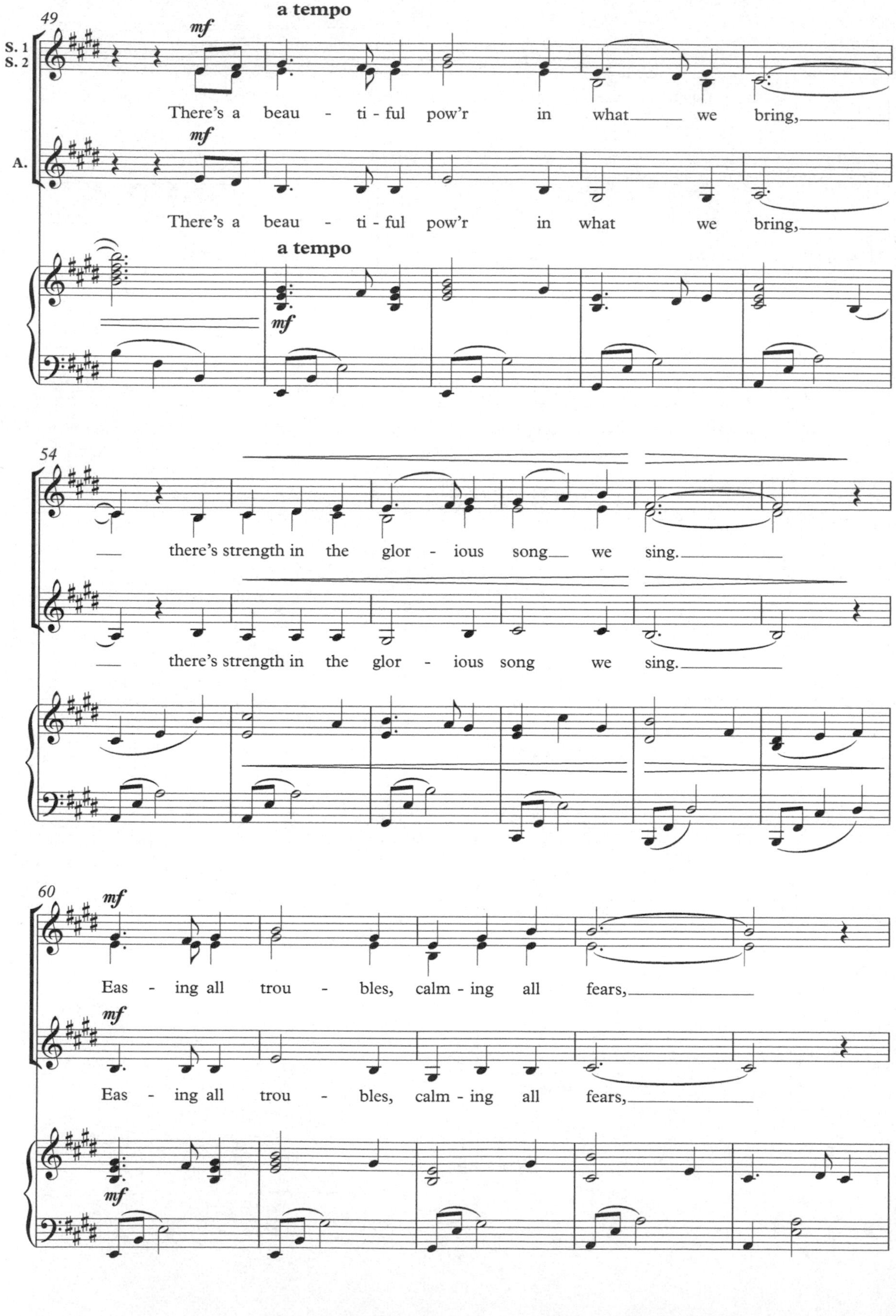
49
a tempo
S. 1
S. 2
mf
There's a beau - ti - ful pow'r in what we bring,
A.
mf
There's a beau - ti - ful pow'r in what we bring,
a tempo
mf
54
there's strength in the glor - ious song we sing.
there's strength in the glor - ious song we sing.
60
mf
Eas - ing all trou - bles, calm - ing all fears,
mf
Eas - ing all trou - bles, calm - ing all fears,
mf

65
joy - ful, with har - mon-ies sing me all the way home with a
joy - ful, with har - mon-ies sing me all the way home with a
71
song in my heart. All the way home
song in my heart. All the way home
77
bright - en my path and car - ry me on, all
bright - en my path and car - ry me on, all
mp
mp
mp

83
the way home.
the way home.
poco meno mosso
89
mf
ah
mf
ah
poco meno mosso
mf
95 unis. p
S. 1
S. 2
Eve - ning brings a shin - ing star, her an - cient an - thems
p

102
p
from a - far.
Si - lence be - low, her song in the sky.
rit.
a tempo
110
f
S. 1
S. 2
Joy - ful with har - mon - ies sing me all the way home with a
A.
Joy - ful with har - mon - ies sing me all the way home with a
rit.
a tempo
f
116
song in my heart. All the way home
song in my heart. All the way home

122
mf
bright-en my path and car - ry me on, all the way
mf
bright-en my path and car - ry me on, all the way
mf
poco rit.
rit.
129
home, all the way
home, all the way
poco rit.
rit.
136
a tempo
molto rit.
mp
home.
mp
home.
a tempo
molto rit.
mp

Commissioned by the Treble Makers Women's Choir and Sharon Little, Chief Treble Maker, to mark their 10th anniversary, their farewell concert, and Canada's 150th anniversary

In time of silver rain

Langston Hughes (1902–67)

SARAH QUARTEL

Duration: 2.5 mins

First performed by the Treble Makers Women's Choir, directed by Sharon Little, at West Lorne United Church, West Lorne, Ontario, on 29 April 2017.

Also available in versions for unison voices and piano (978–0–19–355086–5), SABar and piano (978–0–19–354007–1), and solo voice and piano (high voice 978–0–19–354954–8/low voice 978–0–19–354955–5).

11
f
mf
won - der spreads of life, of life, of life! In
poco rit.
a tempo
14
time of sil - ver rain.
time of sil - ver rain, in time of sil - ver, sil - ver rain.
17
mf
cresc.
In time of sil - ver rain the but - ter - flies lift silk - en wings to
20
poco più mosso
f
catch a rain - bow cry, and trees put forth new leaves to sing, new leaves to

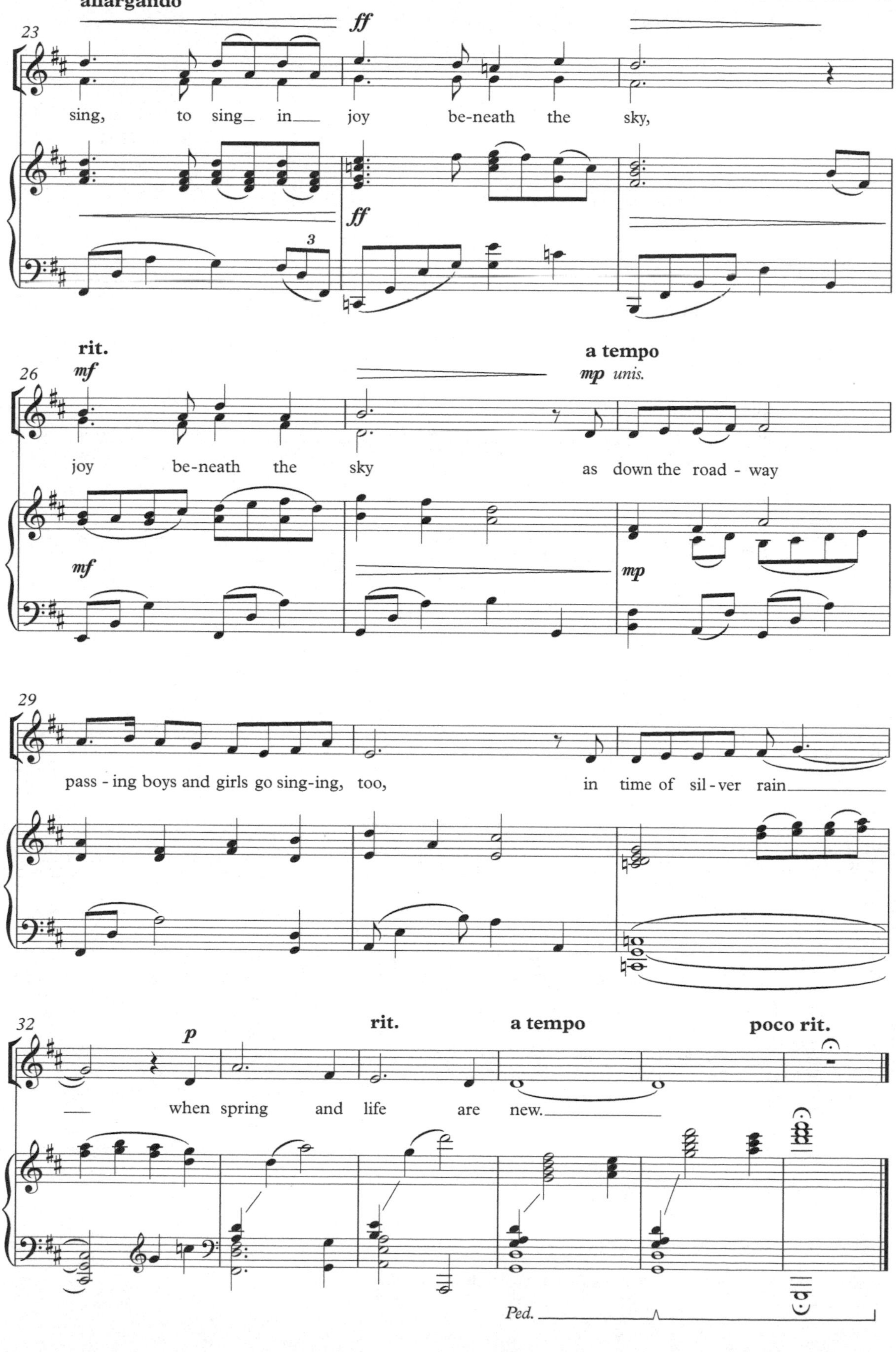
allargando
23
ff
sing, to sing in joy be-neath the sky,
ff
rit.
a tempo
26
mf
mp unis.
joy be-neath the sky as down the road - way
mf
mp
29
pass - ing boys and girls go sing-ing, too, in time of sil - ver rain
32
p
rit.
a tempo
poco rit.
when spring and life are new.
Ped.

Commissioned by Village Voices, Seer Green, Buckinghamshire; Jane Smith, conductor

As you sing

Words and music by
SARAH QUARTEL

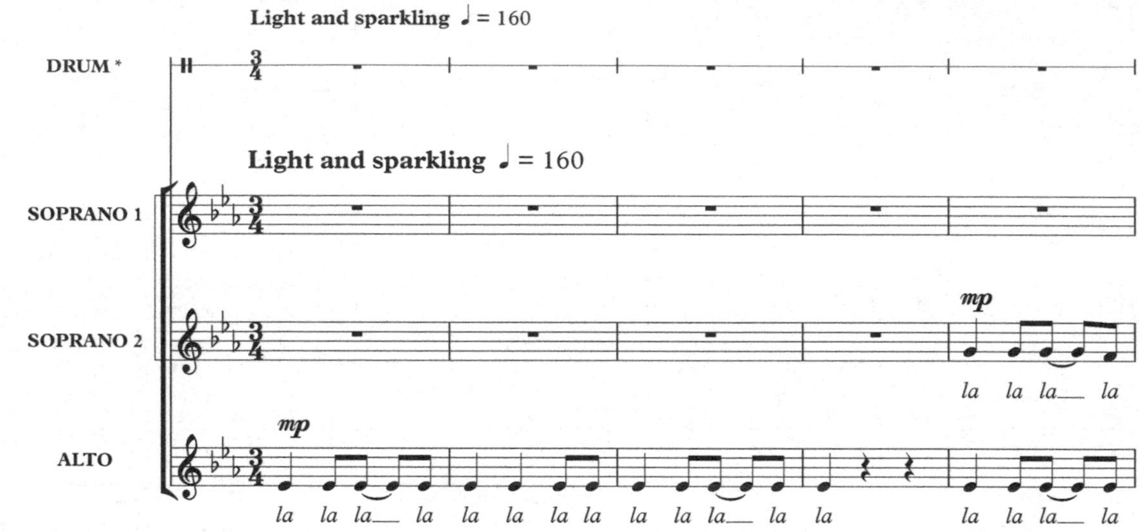

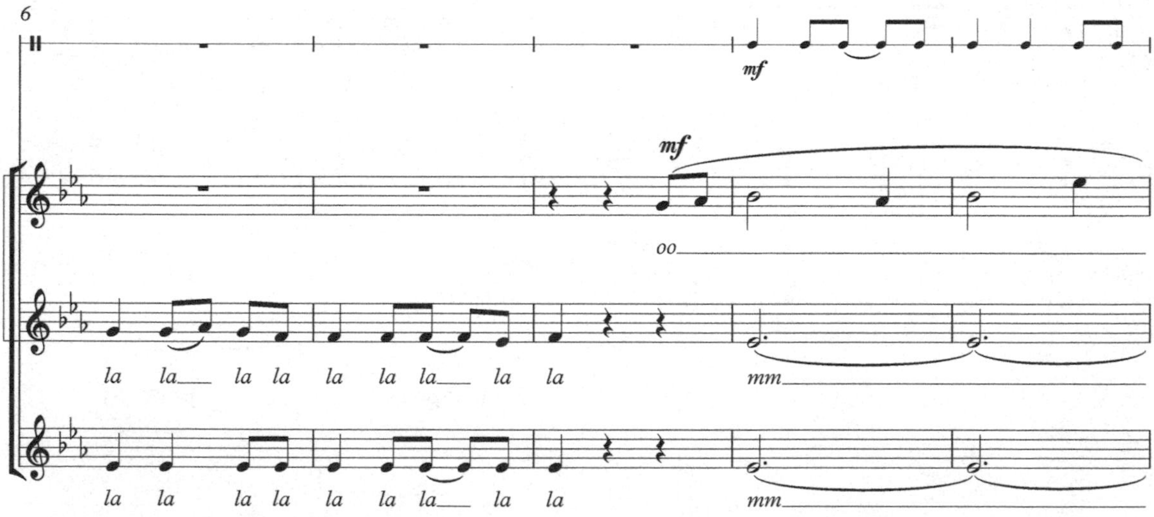

Duration: 3 mins

* Any hand drum with a warm sound.

Originally published in *As you sing* (ISBN 978–0–19–352421–7).

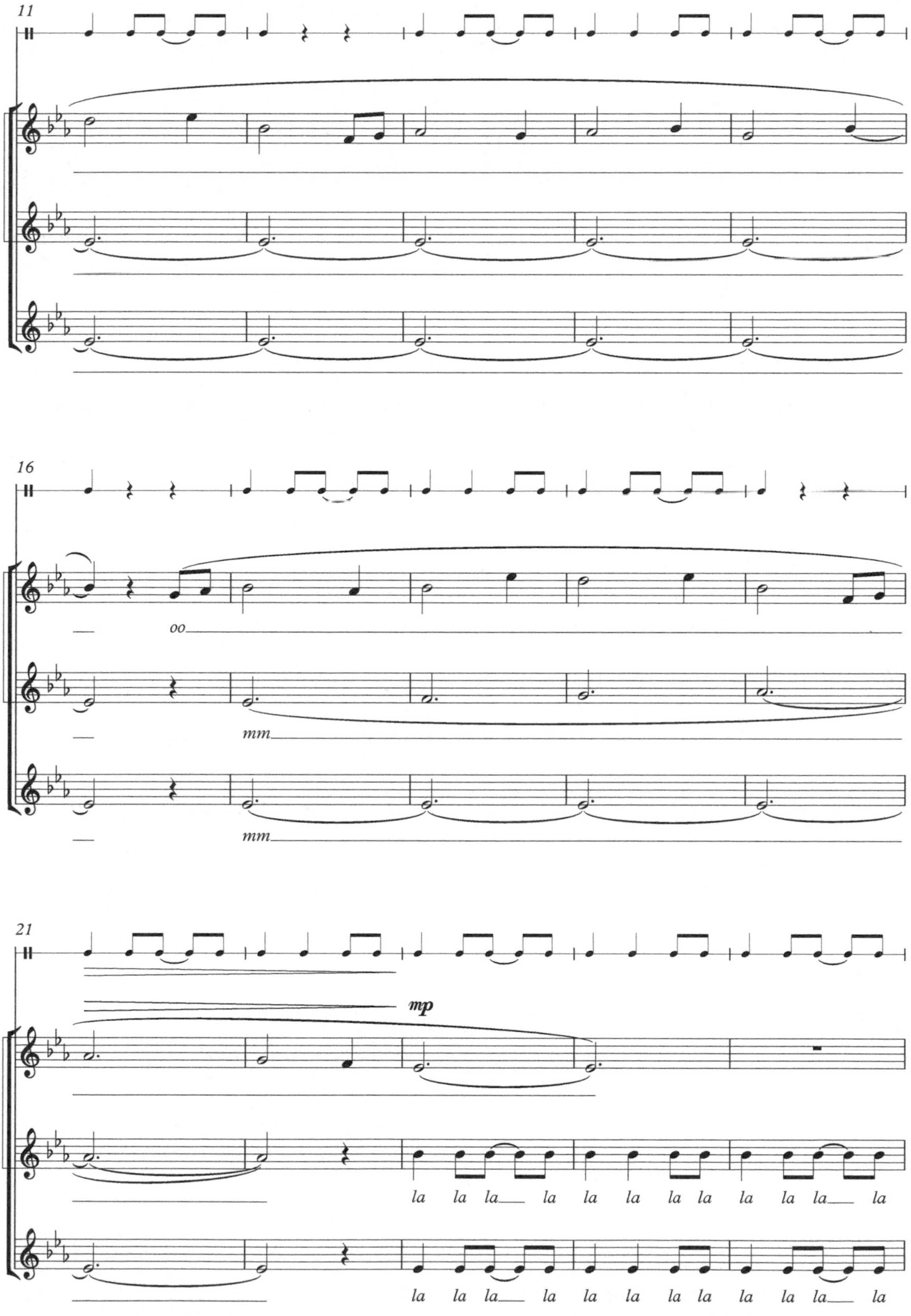
11
16
oo
mm
mm
21
mp
la la la la la la la la la la la la
la la la la la la la la la la la la

26
mf
Your_ voice is like the breath of spring when_
mf
la Your_ voice is like the breath of spring when_
mf
la Your_ voice is like the breath of spring when_
31
first it wakes the flow - ers.___ I___ blos - som bright - ly
first it wakes the flow - ers.___ I___ blos - som bright - ly
first it wakes the flow - ers.___ I___ blos - som bright - ly
37
as you sing, and_ flour - ish by your side.______ And_
as you sing, and_ flour - ish by your side.______
as you sing, and_ flour - ish by your side.______

43
mf
in your sing - ing I am
mp
ah I am
mp
ah I am
49
mp
mp
found. Your voice is like the breath of spring. I flour - ish
p
found. mm
p
found. mm
56
mf
by your side.
mf
la la la la la la la la la la la la la
mf
la la la la la la la la la la la la la

61
mf
la la la la la la la la la la la la la la la la la
la la la la la la la la la la la la la la la la
la la la la la la la la la la la la la
f
Your voice is
66
la la la la la la la la la la la la la la la la la la
la la la la la la la la la la la la la la la la la la
like a cher - ry tree in play - ful bloom be -
71
la la la la la la la la la la la la la la la la la la
la la la la la la la la la la la la la la la la la la
-side me. I dance and flut - ter as you

76
la la la la la la la la la la la la la la la And
la la la la la la la la la la la la la la la And
mf
sing, and shine when you are near. la la
81
f
in your sing - ing I
in your sing - ing I
la la la la la la la la la la la la la la la la la la la la
86
mf
am found. Your voice is like a
mp
am found. la la la la la la la la
mp
la la la la la la la la la la la la la

91
cher - ry tree. I shine when you are near.
la la la la la la la la la
la la la la la la la la la
p
la la la la
96
mp
la la
la la la la la la la
la la la la la la la la la la la
101
f
la la la la la la la la la
la la la la la la la la la la la la la la la
la la la la la la la la la la la la la la

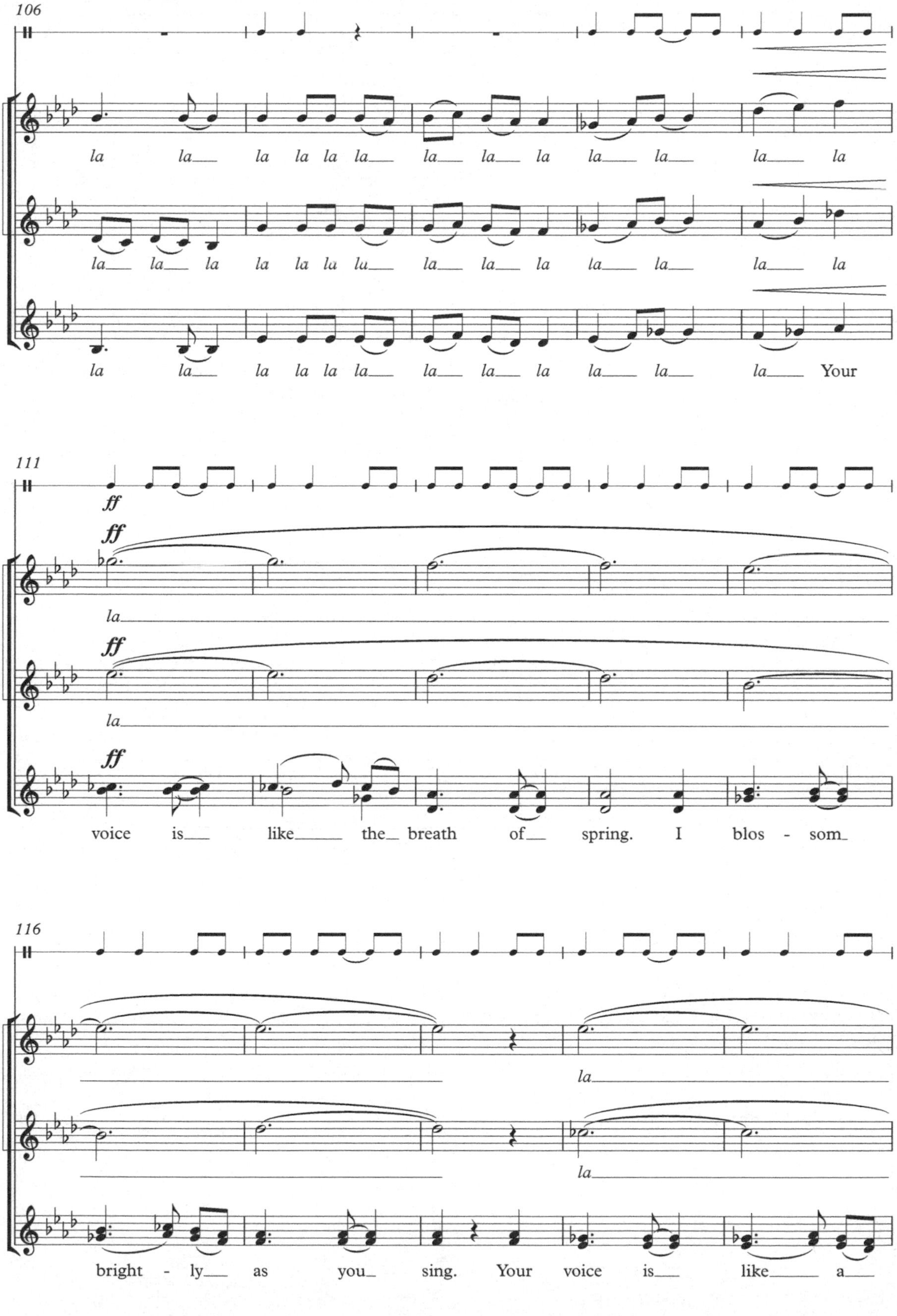
106
la la la la la la la la la la la la la
la la la la la la la la la la la la la
la la la la la la la la la la la Your
111
ff
ff
la
ff
la
ff
voice is like the breath of spring. I blos - som
116
la
la
bright - ly as you sing. Your voice is like a

121
la
la
la
la
cher - ry tree. I shine when you are near.
126
mp
mf
la Your voice is like an an - cient oak that stands in
mp
la
oo
mp
oo
132
gen - tle strength. My roots run deep - er as you sing.
ah
ah

139
mp
f
ah And in your
f
la la la la la la la la la la la la la In your
f
la la la la la la la la la la la la la In your
144
sing - ing I am
sing - ing I am
sing - ing I am
149
mp
mf
found. Your voice is like the breath of spring,
mf
found. Your voice, a
mp
found. mm

155
rit.
rit.
an an - cient oak. You sing me
mp
cher - ry tree, ah
mp
ah
161
a tempo
mf
a tempo
safe - ly home.
mf
la la la la la la la la la la la la
mf
la la la la la la la la la la la la
166
f
f
la la la la la la la la la la la la la la
f
la la la la la la la la la la la la la la
f
la la la la la la la la la la la la la la

Commissioned by the National Children's Chorus, United States of America

All shall be well

Julian of Norwich (1343–after 1416)
Sarah Quartel, inspired by reflections from members
of the commissioning choir submitted in July 2020

SARAH QUARTEL

Duration: 4.5 mins

13
mp
I sing this song for you and in sing - ing heal my -
mp
me. I sing this song for you and in sing - ing heal my -
mp

17
S. 1
mf
- self. Through ev - 'ry dark - ness, ev - 'ry ray of shin-ing light, I
S. 2
mf
- self. Through ev - 'ry dark - ness, ev - 'ry light,
A. 1
A. 2
mf
- self. Through ev - 'ry dark - ness, ev - 'ry light,
mf
Ped.

21
know all shall be well.
all shall be well. oh
all shall be well. oh
25
I sing with love for you and the
I sing with love for you and the,
I sing for you and the,

28
mf
lov - ing fills me. I sing with joy for you
the lov - ing fills me. I sing with joy for you
the lov - ing fills me. I sing for
31
and feel joy - ful-ness my - self. Through ev - 'ry
and feel the joy my - self.
you and feel the joy my - self.

34
dark - - - - - - - - -
mf
— Through ev - 'ry— dark - - - - - -
mf
Ev - - 'ry dark - ness, dark - -
poco rit.
37
f
-ness, through ev - 'ry— ray of shin - ing light,— I know
f
-ness, through ev - 'ry ray— of— light,— I know
f
-ness, through ev - 'ry light, I know
poco rit.
f

41
a tempo
f
all shall be well, shall be well, shall be well,
all shall be well, shall be well, shall be well,
all shall be well, shall be well, shall be well,
a tempo
45
all shall be well, shall be well.
all shall be well, shall be well.
all shall be well, shall be well.

poco rit.
49
f
mf
poco rit.
mf
53
Expansive yet rooted ♩ = 84
mp
mp
In be - ing o - pen and giv - ing I see the beau - ty a - round me.
p
hmm
p
hmm
Expansive yet rooted ♩ = 84
8va
8va
mp
8vb
8vb
Ped.

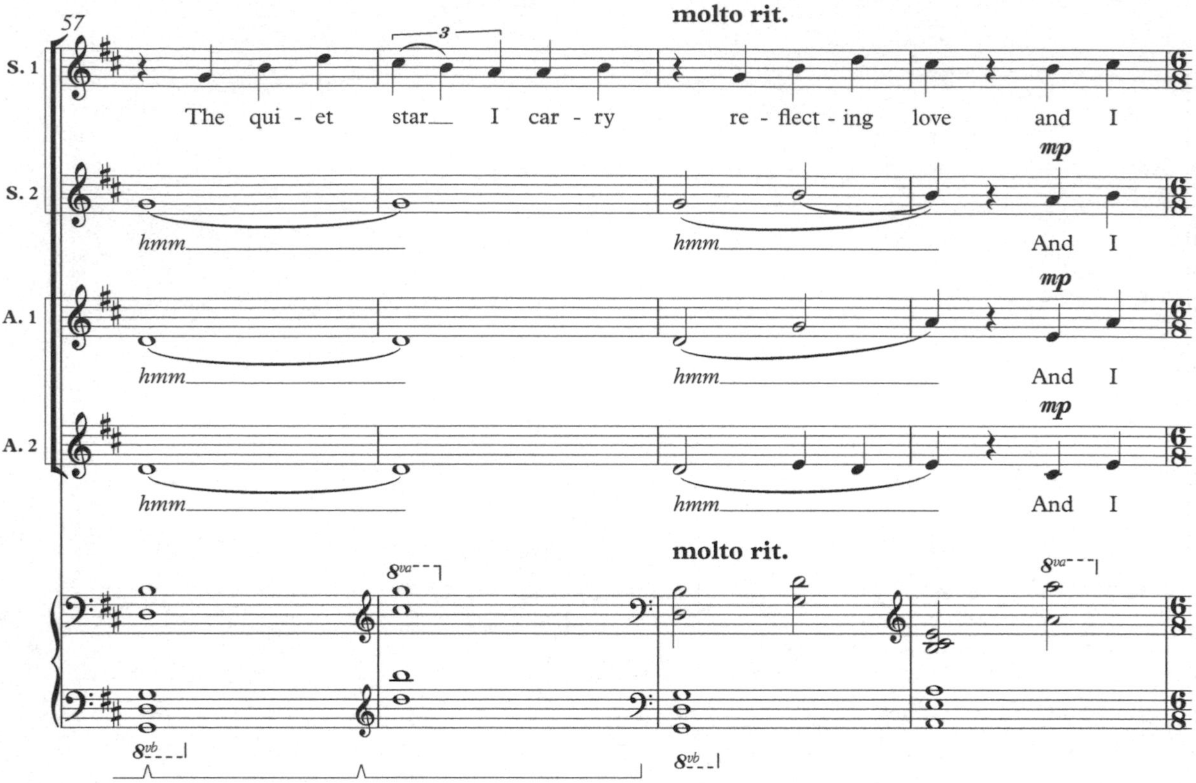
57
molto rit.
S. 1
The qui - et star I car - ry re - flect - ing love and I
S. 2
hmm
hmm
mp
And I
A. 1
hmm
hmm
mp
And I
A. 2
hmm
hmm
mp
And I
molto rit.

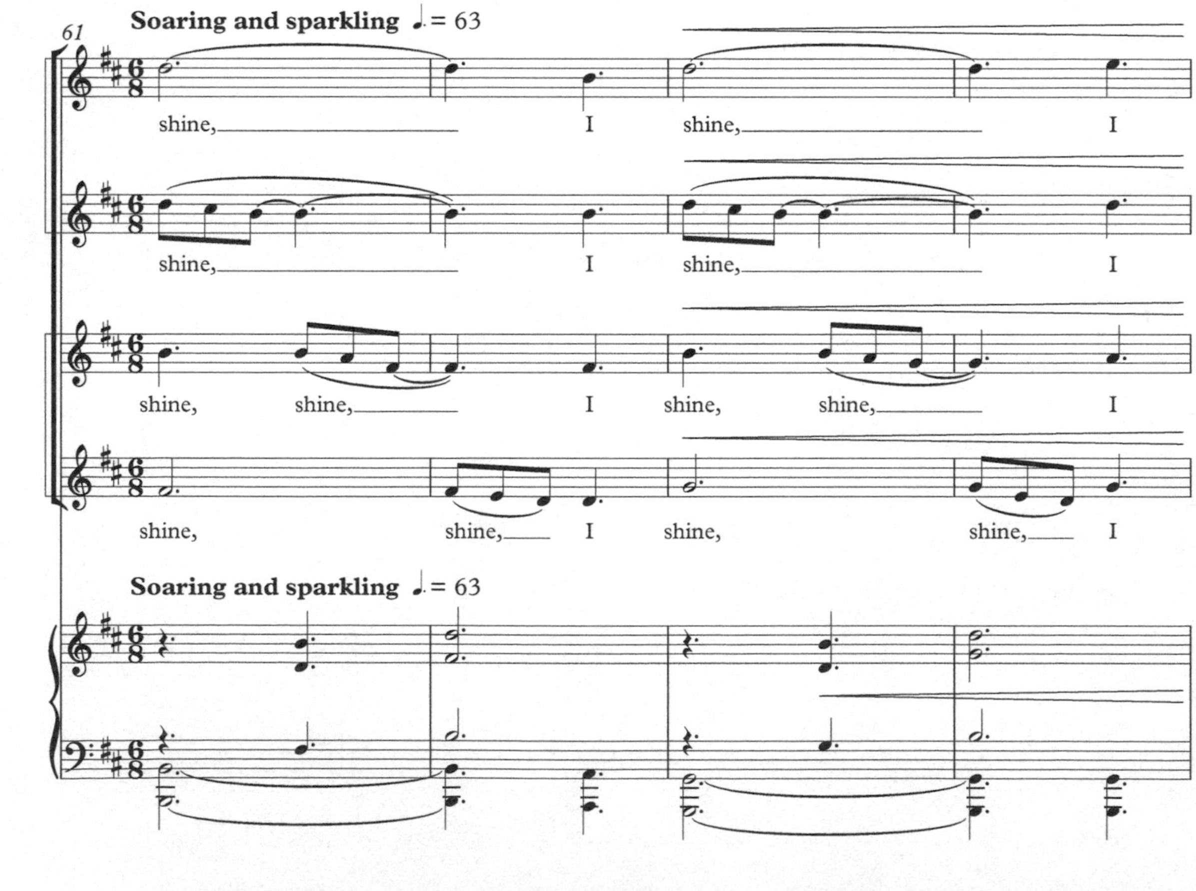
61
Soaring and sparkling ♩. = 63
shine, I shine, I
shine, I shine, I
shine, shine, I shine, shine, I
shine, shine, I shine, shine, I
Soaring and sparkling ♩. = 63

65
mf
shine, I shine, I
shine, I shine, I
shine, shine, I shine, shine, I
shine, shine, I shine, shine, I
69
mp
shine, I shine, I
shine, I shine, I
shine, shine, I shine, shine, I
shine, shine, I shine, shine, I

73
mf
shine, I shine, I
mf
shine, I shine, I
mf
shine, shine, I shine, shine, I
mf
shine, shine, I shine, shine, I
mf
77
rit.
mp
cresc.
shine, shine, shine!
mp
cresc.
shine, shine, shine, shine!
mp
cresc.
shine, I shine, I shine, I shine!
mp
cresc.
shine, shine, shine, shine!
rit.
mp
cresc.

Confirmed and glad ♩. = 69
81
f
All shall be well, shall be
All shall be well, shall be
All shall be well, shall be
All shall be well, shall be
Confirmed and glad ♩. = 69
85
mf
well, shall be well,
well, shall be well,
well, shall be well,
well, shall be well,

89
f
all shall be well, shall be
all shall be well, shall be
all shall be well, shall be
all shall be well, shall be
93
S. 1
S. 2
well.
A. 1
A. 2
well.

97
f
f
101
mf
S. 1
mp
I
mp
105
(mf)
S. 1
give this song to you, I give this song to you, I
mf
S. 2
mp
I give this song to you, I give this song to
ALTOS unis.
A. 1
A. 2
mp
I give this song to you, I give this

109
mp
give this song to you, I give this song to you, to
mf
you, I give this song to you, I give this song to
mf
song to you, I give this song to you, this song to
mf
113
rit.
mp
you.
mp
you.
mp
you.
rit.
mp
Ped.

Commissioned by the National Children's Chorus, United States of America

All shall be well

Julian of Norwich (1343–after 1416)
Sarah Quartel, inspired by reflections from members
of the commissioning choir submitted in July 2020

SARAH QUARTEL

Duration: 4.5 mins

a tempo
41
f
45
poco rit.
49
f
3
mf
Expansive, yet rooted ♩ = 84
molto rit.
52
5
2
mp
Soaring and sparkling ♩. = 63
61
4
SOPRANO 1
shine,
I
shine,
I
mf
70
2
2
75
rit.
Confirmed and glad ♩. = 69
79
f

83
mf
87
f
92
96
f
102
mf
(mf)
108
rit.
113
mp

Commissioned by The Richmond Singers, Richmond, British Columbia,
Natasha Neufeld, Artistic Director

Sing, my Child

Words and music by
SARAH QUARTEL

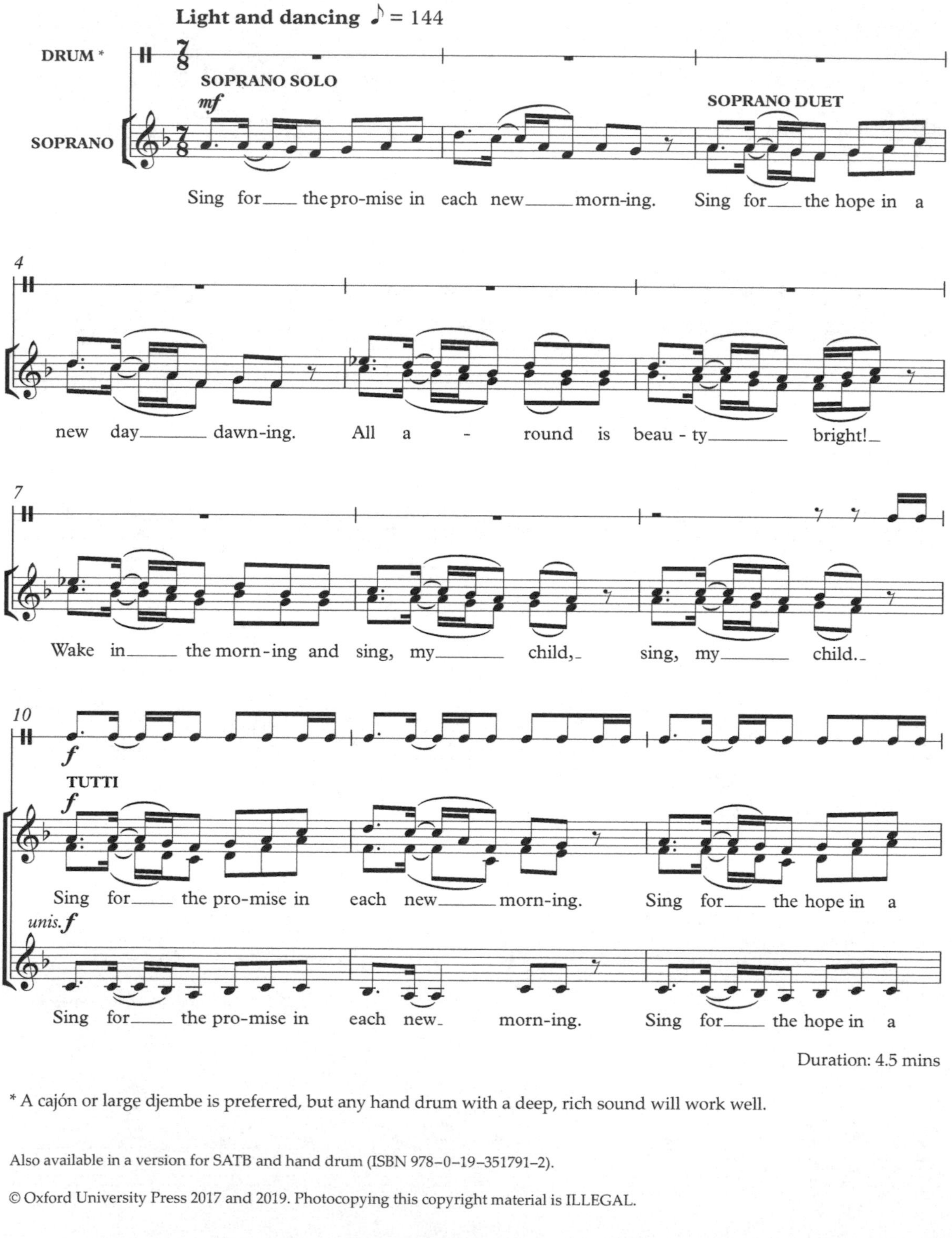

Duration: 4.5 mins

* A cajón or large djembe is preferred, but any hand drum with a deep, rich sound will work well.

Also available in a version for SATB and hand drum (ISBN 978–0–19–351791–2).

13
new day dawn-ing. All a - round is beau - ty bright!
new day dawn-ing. All a - round is beau - ty bright!
16
Wake in the morn-ing and sing, my child, sing, my child,
Wake in the morn-ing and sing, my child, sing, my child,
19
sub. p
mf
sing, my child, sing, my child,
sing, my child, oh sing, my child, oh sing, my child, oh sing, my child, oh
23
p
sing, my child. ah
sing, my child, oh sing, my child, oh sing, my child, oh sing, my child.

27
f
f
Dance in the joy of the day un - fold-ing. Dance as you work and
unis. f
Dance in the joy of the day un - fold-ing. Dance as you work and
30
dance as you're learn-ing. All a - round is beau - ty bright!
dance as you're learn-ing. All a - round is beau - ty bright!
33
Take in the day and dance, my child, dance, my child,
Take in the day and dance, my child, dance, my child,

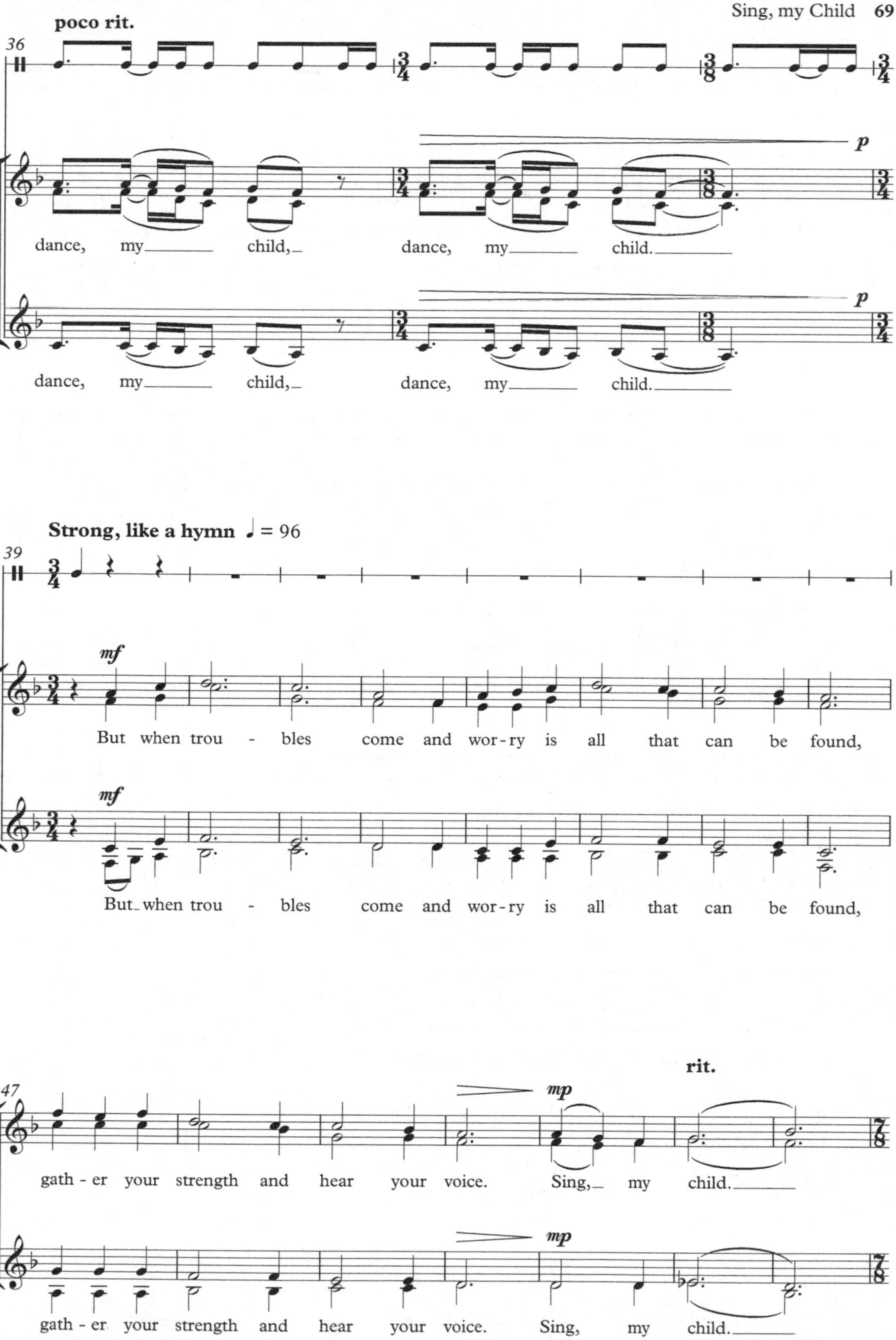
poco rit.
36
dance, my child, dance, my child.
p
dance, my child, dance, my child.
Strong, like a hymn ♩ = 96
39
mf
But when trou - bles come and wor-ry is all that can be found,
But when trou - bles come and wor-ry is all that can be found,
47
rit.
mp
gath - er your strength and hear your voice. Sing, my child.
gath - er your strength and hear your voice. Sing, my child.

Tempo I ♪ = 144
D.
Laugh in the cool and the fresh of the ev'n-ing. Laugh in your tri - umph,
Laugh, laugh, oh laugh, my child, laugh, laugh, oh laugh, my child, laugh, laugh, oh laugh, my child,
laugh in suc-ceed-ing. All a - round is beau - ty bright!
laugh, laugh, oh laugh, my child, laugh, laugh, oh laugh, my child, laugh, laugh, oh laugh, my child,
Peace in the still-ness and
Rest in the ev'n-ing and laugh, my child.
Peace,
laugh, laugh, oh laugh, my child, laugh, laugh, my child.
Peace,
dark of the night. Peace in the dreams of your si - lent de - lights.
peace, peace, peace,
peace, peace, peace,

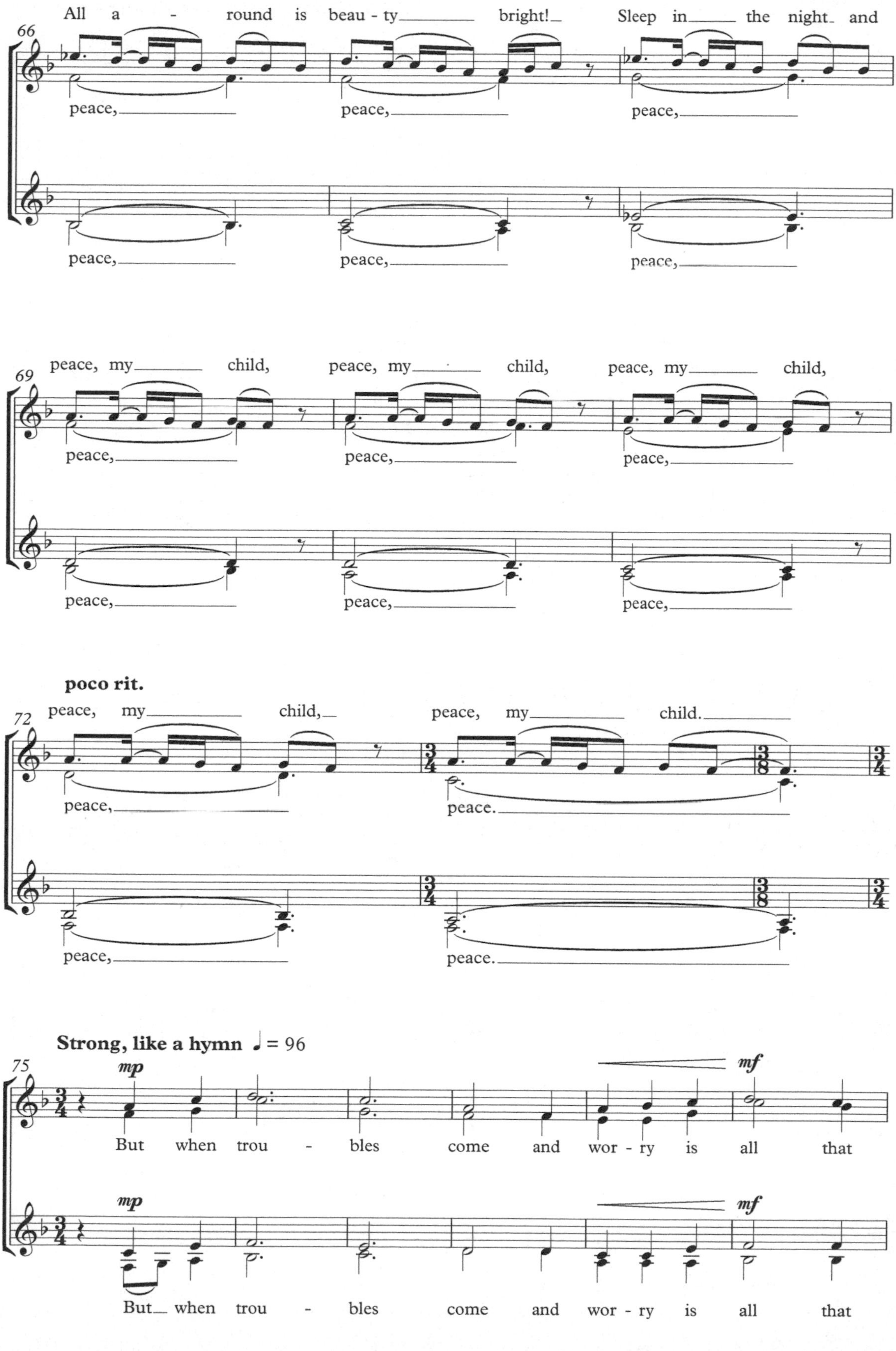
All a - round is beau - ty bright! Sleep in the night and
66
peace, peace, peace,
peace, peace, peace,
peace, my child, peace, my child, peace, my child,
69
peace, peace, peace,
peace, peace, peace,
poco rit.
peace, my child, peace, my child.
72
peace, peace.
peace, peace.
Strong, like a hymn ♩ = 96
75
mp
mf
But when trou - bles come and wor - ry is all that
mp
mf
But when trou - bles come and wor - ry is all that

81
f
can be found, gath - er your strength and hear your voice.
f
can be found, gath - er your strength and hear your voice.
87
mp
mf
Sing, my child. Dance, my child.
mp
mf
Sing my child. Dance, my child.
95
f
sub. p
Laugh, my child. Peace, my child.
f
sub. p
Laugh, my child. Peace, my child.
SOPRANO DUET
rit.
104
mp
Peace, my child, oh, peace, my child.
p
oo
oo
p
oo
oo

Commissioned by the Atlanta Women's Chorus,
Dr Melissa Arasi, Artistic Director

Refuge

Sara Teasdale (1884–1933)

SARAH QUARTEL

Duration: 3 mins

10
mf
turned to sand sift - ing through my close - clenched hand,
mf
13
mp
from my own fault's sla - ver - y, if I can sing, I
mp
poco accel.
warm and hopeful ♩ = 76
16
S. 1/2
mf
still am free.
For with my sing-ing I can
A.
mf
still am free.
For with my sing-ing I can
poco accel.
warm and hopeful ♩ = 76
mf

19
mp
make a re-fuge for my spi-rit's sake,
mp
make a re-fuge for my spi-rit's sake,
mp
a house of shi - ning words,
22
mf
mp
a house of shi - ning words to be my fra-gile im - mor -
mf
mp
a house of shi - ning words to be my fra-gile im - mor -
mf
mp

25
-tal - i - ty.
If I can sing,
-tal - i - ty.
3
I still am
29
mf
if I can sing,
p
if I can sing,
mf
3
free,
I still am
free,
p
I still am
mf
p

32
mp
if I can sing, if I can sing, if I can sing,
mp
free, I still am free, I still am free, I still am
mp

35
mf
f
if I can sing, if I can sing, if I can sing,
mf
f
free, I still am free, I still am free, I still am
mf
f

38
if I can sing.
For with my sing-ing I can make a
free.
For with my sing-ing I can make a

41
a house of shi - ning
mf
re-fuge for my spi-rit's sake,
a house of shi - ning
mf
re-fuge for my spi-rit's sake,
a house of shi - ning
mf

words,
44
f
words, to be a re - fuge, a
f
words, to be a re - fuge, a
f

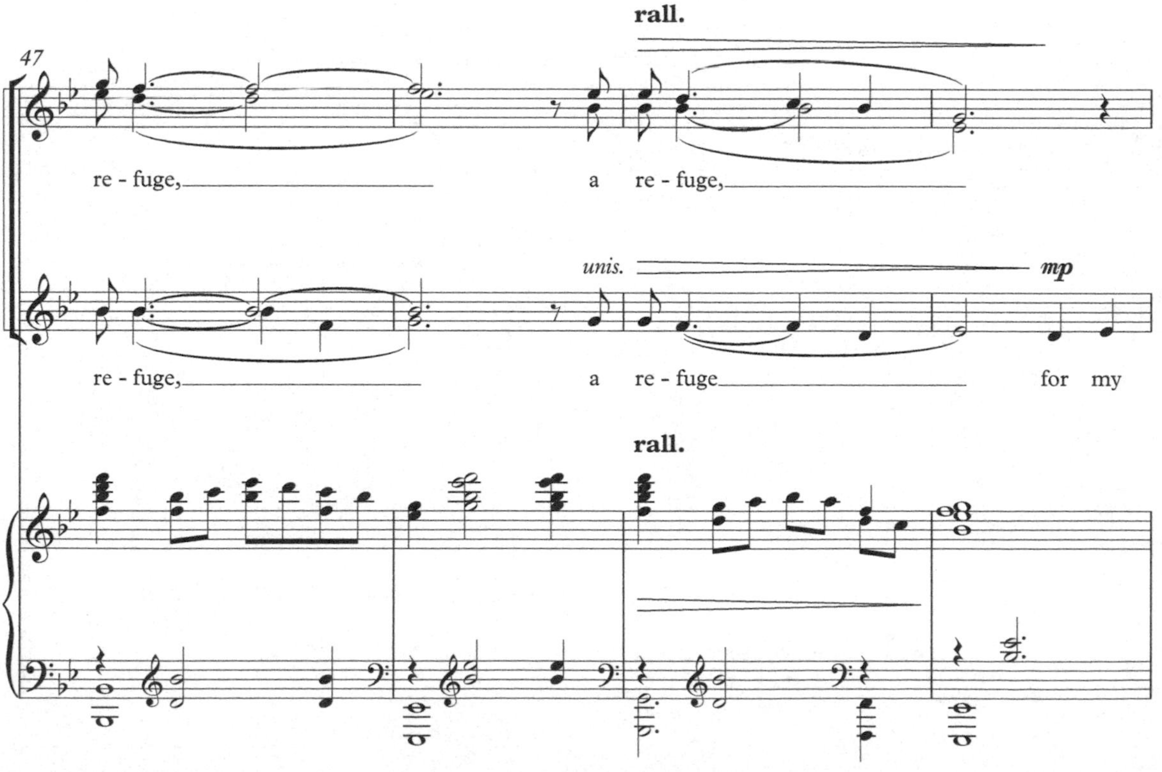
rall.
47
re - fuge, a re - fuge,
unis.
mp
re - fuge, a re - fuge for my
rall.

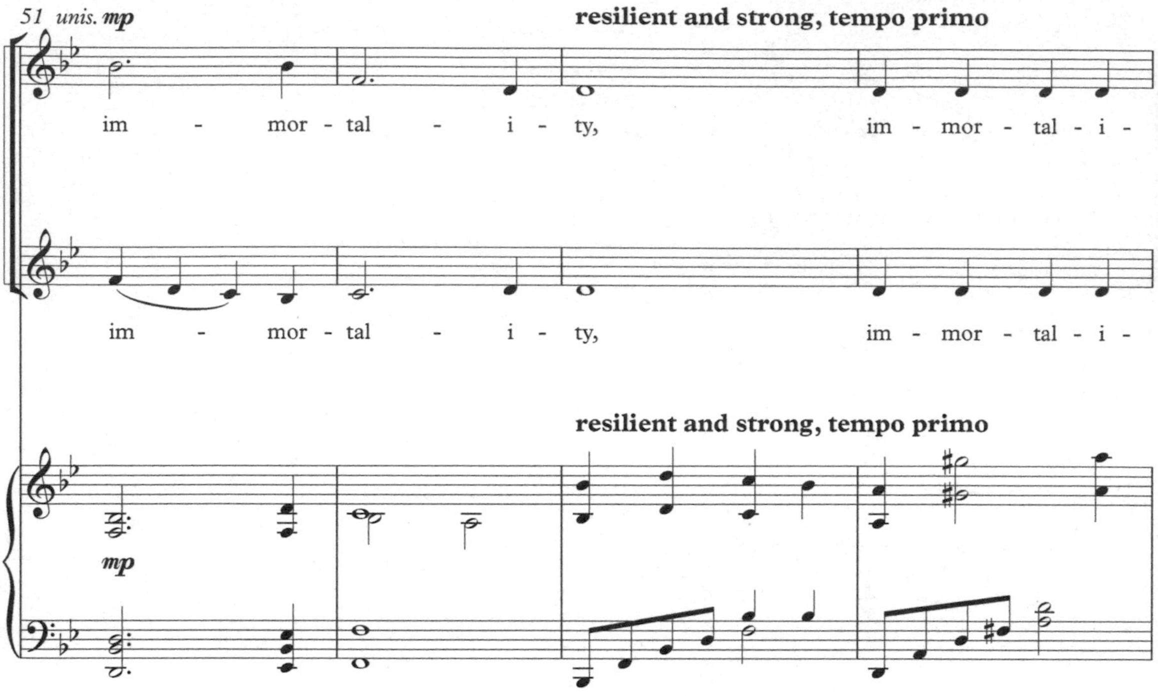
51 unis. mp
resilient and strong, tempo primo
im - mor - tal - i - ty, im - mor - tal - i -
im - mor - tal - i - ty, im - mor - tal - i -
resilient and strong, tempo primo
mp

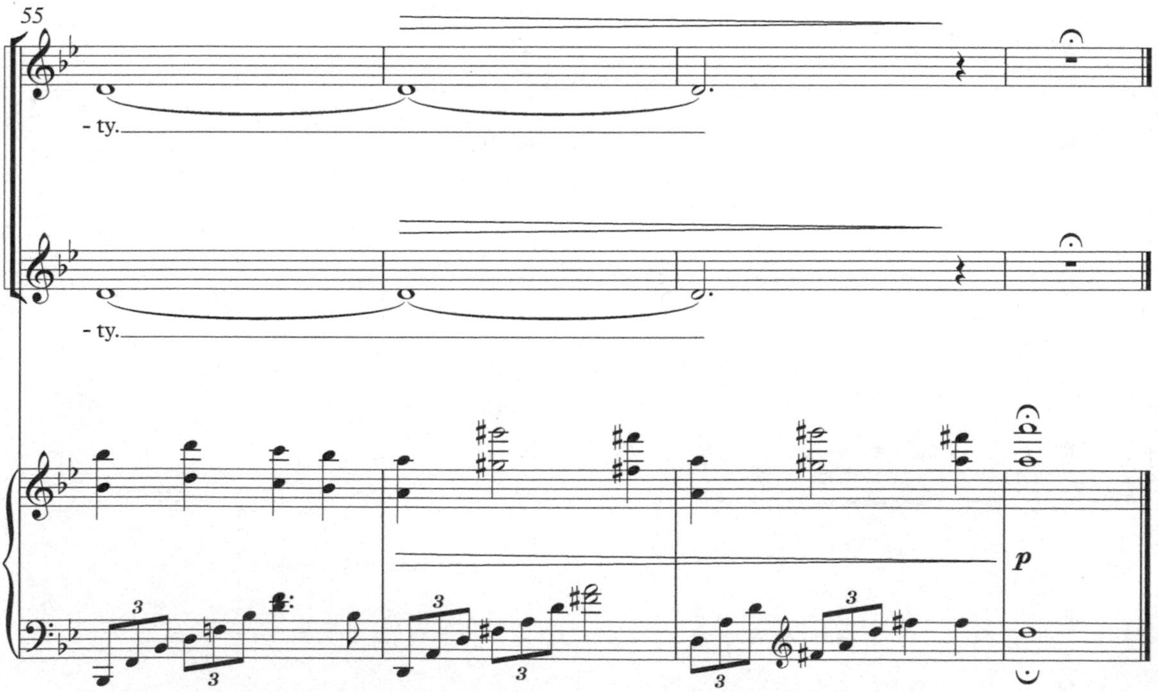
55
- ty.
- ty.
p

Commissioned by the Peninsula Girls Chorus of Burlingame, California, and their Artistic Director Karyn Silva to celebrate 20 years of providing a place where girls find their voices

Voice on the Wind

Words and music by
SARAH QUARTEL

Duration: 4 mins

* Alternatively a bodhrán may be used.

Also available in a version for SATB and hand drum (978–0–19–352587–0).

17
S. 1/2
A. 1/2
mp
I heard a voice on the sum-mer wind,
hoo wah hoo wah hoo
20
Blow-ing free and blow-ing wild.
23
hoo wah hoo wah hoo wah hoo
mf
I heard a voice on the sum-mer wind,
26
hoo wah hoo wah hoo

29
S. 1
Strength and spi - rit in her song.
S. 2
Strength and spi - rit in her song.
. 1/2
Strength and spi - rit in her song.
31
hoo wah hoo wah hoo wah hoo
hoo wah hoo wah hoo wah hoo
hoo wah hoo wah hoo wah hoo
33
hoo wah hoo wah hoo wah hoo hoo wah hoo wah hoo
hoo wah ya hoo wah ya
hoo wah ya hoo wah ya

35
f
hoo wah hoo wah hoo wah hoo hoo wah hoo wah hoo
hoo wah ya hoo wah ya
hoo wah ya hoo wah ya
37
Strength and spi - rit in her song.
hoo wah ya hoo wah ya
hoo wah ya hoo wah ya
39
mp
hoo wah hoo wah hoo wah hoo dun dun dun
hoo wah ya hoo wah ya dun dun dun
hoo wah ya hoo wah ya dun dun dun

42
mf
dun
dun
I heard a voice on the sum-mer wind,
dun
dun
dun
I heard a voice on the sum-mer wind,
dun
dun
dun
I heard a voice on the sum-mer wind,
44
mf
hoo wah hoo wah hoo
hoo wah hoo wah hoo
hoo wah hoo wah hoo
47
With a song I seem to know.
hoo wah hoo wah hoo wah hoo
With a song I seem to know.
hoo wah hoo wah hoo wah hoo
With a song I seem to know.
hoo wah hoo wah hoo wah hoo

50
I heard a voice on the sum - mer wind,
I heard a voice on the sum - mer wind,
I heard a voice on the sum - mer wind,
52
hoo wah hoo wah hoo wah
hoo wah hoo wah hoo wah
hoo wah hoo wah hoo wah
55
Sounds fa - mil - iar like my own.
Sounds fa - mil - iar like my own.
Sounds fa - mil - iar like my own.

57
mf
f
S. 1
S. 2
A. 1
A. 2
mp
p
hoo wah hoo wah hoo wah hoo hoo
hoo wah hoo wah hoo wah hoo hoo wah hoo wah hoo
hoo wah hoo wah hoo wah hoo hoo wah hoo wah hoo wah hoo
hoo wah hoo wah hoo
59
A. 1
A. 2
hoo wah ya hoo wah
hoo wah hoo wah hoo wah hoo hoo wah hoo wah hoo
hoo wah
hoo wah ya hoo wah ya
61
hoo wah ya hoo wah
hoo wah hoo wah hoo wah hoo hoo wah hoo wah hoo
hoo wah
hoo wah ya hoo wah ya

63
p
Sounds fa - mil - iar like my own.
p
hoo wah ya hoo wah ya
hoo wah ya hoo wah ya
65
p
mp
mp
hoo wah oh wah oo
mp
mf
hoo wah I heard a voice on the
p
mp
dun dun dun dun dun dun oo
68
wah oh
sum - mer wind, on the sum - mer wind, on the sum - mer wind,
wah oh

71
oo
wah
oh
Moves me like she knows me well, she knows me well, she
oo
wah
oh
74
oo
wah
knows me well. I heard a voice on the summer wind, on the
oo
wah
77
mf
oh
oo
sum - mer wind, on the sum - mer wind, Sounds fa - mil - iar
I heard a voice on the sum - mer wind,
mf
oh
oo

80
wah
oh
like my own.
wah
oh
Rooted and confident ♩ = 66
83
S. 1/2
I am the voice on the sum - mer wind, hoo wah hoo wah
A. 1/2
I am the voice on the sum - mer wind, hoo wah hoo wah
89
rit.
hoo Strong and sure where - e'er I stand.
hoo Strong and sure where - e'er I stand.
Strong and driving to the end ♩ = 104
95
S. 1
hoo wah hoo wah hoo wah hoo hoo wah ya
S. 2
hoo wah hoo wah hoo wah hoo hoo wah hoo wah hoo wah hoo
A. 1/2
hoo wah hoo wah hoo wah hoo hoo wah ya

97
hoo wah___ hoo wah___ ya
hoo wah_ hoo wah hoo hoo wah_ hoo wah hoo wah hoo
hoo wah___
hoo wah___ ya hoo wah___ ya
99
hoo wah___ I am the
hoo wah hoo wah hoo I am the
hoo wa___
hoo wah___ ya I am the
102
ff
voice.___ hoo wah hoo wah hoo wah hoo
voice.___ hoo wah hoo wah hoo wah hoo
voice.___ hoo wah hoo wah hoo wah hoo